HBJ HEALTH

Blue

Consulting Health Educators

Molly Kay Berger, R.N.
School Nurse/Health Educator
Houston Independent School District
Houston, Texas

Barbara A. Galpin
Teacher of Health and Physical
*   Education*
Islip Public Schools
Islip, New York

Kathleen Middleton
Director of Curriculum
National Center for Health Education
San Francisco, California

Judith K. Scheer
Formerly Associate Professor
Department of Health Education
The University of Toledo
Toledo, Ohio

Joel B. Shapiro
Teacher of Elementary School Health
*   and Physical Education*
Community School District 10
Bronx, New York

Nancy L. Young
Classroom Teacher and Supervisor of
*   Student Teachers*
Royerton Elementary School
Muncie, Indiana

Consulting Health Specialists

Barbara L. Flye, Ph. D.
Director of Clinical Services
Andrus Home for Children
Yonkers, New York

Janice Gilyard-Robinson, R.N.
Assistant Professor and
*   Pediatric Nurse Specialist*
School of Nursing
The University of North Carolina
*   at Greensboro*

Wesley Halpert, D.D.S.
Clinical Professor of Dentistry
Columbia University School of Dental
*   and Oral Surgery*
New York, New York

Irwin Rappaport, M.D., F.A.A.P.
Clinical Associate Professor of Pediatrics
Director, Allergy and Immunology
Department of Pediatrics
The New York Hospital
Cornell University Medical Center
New York, New York

Consulting Reading Specialists

Marjorie Slavick Frank
Specialist in Reading and
*   Language Development*
Brooklyn, New York

P. J. Hutchins
Supervisor
Bureau of Reading Education
New York State Education Department
New York, New York

HBJ HARCOURT BRACE JOVANOVICH, PUBLISHERS
Orlando   New York   Chicago   San Diego   Atlanta   Dallas

Printed in the United States of America

ISBN 0-15-369100-X

EDITORIAL DEVELOPMENT: M & H Ideas, Inc., under the
supervision of the HBJ Health Editorial Department

PRODUCTION MANAGEMENT: Elaine Walling

DESIGN AND ART DIRECTION: Taurins Design Associates

COVER CREDIT
Monkmeyer Press Photo, © Hugh Rogers

PHOTOGRAPH ACKNOWLEDGMENTS
KEY: T, Top; B, Bottom; L, Left; C, Center; R, Right.

HBJ PHOTOS by James Gilmour: 38, 39, 44, 50, 92, 93, 122, 123.
HBJ PHOTOS by Rosmarie Hausherr: 4, 5, 6, 8, 9, 13, 14, 15,
16, 20-21, 24R, 28L, 40, 41, 46, 49TR, 49BR, 54-55, 56, 59, 66,
72R, 73, 74, 75, 84, 91, 94, 98, 99, 110, 111, 114, 115L, 118R,
119, 130, 138, 145T and BL, 146, 147, 148, 149BL and BR.
HBJ PHOTOS by Ken Lax: 2-3, 22, 29, 30, 31, 36-37, 47, 49L,
58, 62, 63, 64, 70-71, 76, 77, 78, 79, 82, 83, 88-89, 90, 95,
104-105, 106, 107, 108-109, 115TR, 116, 117, 118L, 120, 121,
128-129, 131, 133, 134, 135, 139, 140, 145BR, 149TL and TR.

PHOTO LOCATION COORDINATORS: Lynn Croton, Susan
Wechsler.

RESEARCH CREDITS: The Image Bank, © Whitney L. Lane: 7.
Monkmeyer Press Photo Service, © Hugh Rogers: 12. H.
Armstrong Roberts: 24L. Monkmeyer Press Photo Service, ©
Mimi Forsyth: 25L. The Image Bank, © Benn Mitchell: 25R.
Shostal Associates, © John Wang: 28. DPI, © Dunn: 45. H.
Armstrong Roberts: 65. Photo Researchers, Inc., © Richard
Hutchings: 72L. Phototake, © Martin M. Rotker: 85. Land-
slides, © Alex S. MacLean: 132.

PHOTO RESEARCHER: Aija Klebers, Taurins Design
Associates, Inc.

ART ACKNOWLEDGMENTS
Teresa Anderko: 67, 93, 141. Susan Blubaugh: 51, 85. Gwen
Connelly: 32, 33, 100, 101. Carol Ann Morley: 23, 57. Marti
Shohet: 124, 125. Jerry Smath: 10, 11, 26, 27, 42, 43, 48, 52,
53, 60, 61, 80, 81, 97, 112, 113, 136, 137, all "Do You Remem-
ber" chalk boards, and all "Health Check-Up" toucans. Valerie
Smath: 78 poster. Lane Yerkes: 17.

CONTENTS

CHAPTER 1

You and Other People

In some ways we are different.
In some ways we are the same.
We can get along with others.
It feels good to get along.
How can we get along?

Health Words

special
feelings
habits
friends
family

You Are Special

There is no one just like you.
No one looks just like you.
No one acts just like you do.
No one can take your place.
You are special.

Look at all five pictures.

Tell how the children are special.

Tell why you are special.

How does it feel to be special?

Having Feelings

Everyone has feelings.

You may like some of your feelings.

You may not like others.

All your feelings are important.

They are part of you.

They are special.

They help make you special.

Look at both pictures.

Tell who is happy.

Why might that person be happy?

Name a feeling you like to have.

Show the feeling.

Name some other feelings.

Tell why feelings are important.

Feeling Good About Yourself

Good health is many things.

It is being well.

It is feeling good inside.

Good habits help you feel good.

Run and play.

Eat right.

Get the rest and sleep you need.

Care about how you look.

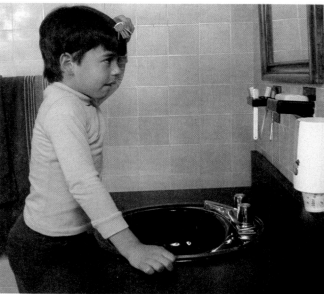

Look at all four pictures.

Name the good health habits.

Tell why they are important.

Tell about other good health habits.

Tell why these habits are important.

Health Highlight

Guess the Feelings

1. Mommy hugged me,
Nice and tight.
She kissed me.
Then, she said, "Good night."

2. We said, "So long."
I waved good-bye.
Then, a teardrop
Filled my eye.

3. I laughed and danced.
I gave a shout.
I hopped and jumped.
I skipped about.

Going, Seeing, and Doing

1. Hop like a rabbit.
   Jump like a frog.
   Run like a cat.
   How do you feel?

2. Look around you.
   How many have brown hair?
   How many have blue eyes?

3. Show a feeling.
   Use your face.
   Use your body.
   See if others can guess.

Being a Friend

Friends care about each other.
They help when they can.
They share when they can.
Friends have fun together.
It feels good to have friends.
It feels good to be a friend.

Look at both pictures.

Are the children friends?

How can you tell?

Tell more ways to be a friend.

Caring About Others

All of us need help sometimes.

You can help your family.

You can help others.

Helping can be fun.

It feels good to help.

It feels good to be helped.

Look at all five pictures.

Tell how the children are helping.

Tell about other ways to help.

How does it feel to help?

Your Turn

New in School

Sandy is new in school.
She doesn't know where to go.
She doesn't know what to do.
She feels all alone.

Help Sandy feel better.
Tell what you would do.
Tell how your ideas would help.

Health in Action

1. Write a letter.
   Write to a friend.
   Say something nice.
   How will your friend feel?

2. Make a doll.
   Teach it a good health habit.
   Set a good example.

3. Plan ways to help at home.
   Make a list of the ways.
   Help at home every day.

4. Copy the chart.
   Write in each box.
   Tell how you feel.

before lunch	
after lunch	
at bedtime	

Do You Remember?

Your Health Words

Finish the sentences.
Use the Health Words.

1. I live with my ___.
2. Happy and sad are ___.
3. Resting is a good health ___.

Your Health Ideas

1. Tell a way people are special.
2. Name some different feelings.
3. Tell about some ways to be a friend.

Health Check-Up

Answer "Yes" or "No."

1. Are just a few people special?
2. Is everyone different?
3. Does it feel good to be happy?
4. Does it feel good to be sad?
5. Is exercise a good health habit?
6. Is sleep part of good health?
7. Do friends share?
8. Is helping part of good health?

CHAPTER 2

Growing

You grow in many ways.

Some you can see.

Some you cannot.

You can help yourself grow.

Others can help you, too.

In what ways do you grow?

Health Words

growing

body

learning

exercise

OCT

MAY

NOVEMBER

21

Getting Bigger

Once you were very small.
Now, you are not so small.
You are growing.
Your hands and feet are bigger.
So are your arms and legs.
Your body grows in many ways.

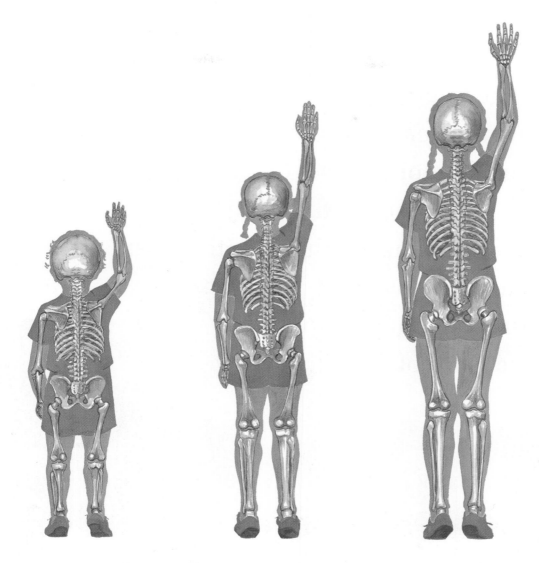

Look at the pictures on page 22.

What kind of growing do they show?

Look at the pictures on this page.

What kind of growing do they show?

Name other parts of you that grow.

Growing Up

You are growing up.

You are learning new things.

You are doing new things.

You do some of them yourself.

You do some of them with others.

These are ways of growing up.

Growing up is important.

It is part of being healthy.

Look at the pictures on page 24.

The same boy is in both pictures.

How has he grown up?

Look at the pictures on this page.

Tell how the children are growing up.

Tell other ways of growing up.

Health Highlight

How Are You Growing?

Read each sentence.

Each one tells about growing.

Tell the kind of growing.

Your teeth are growing.

You help others.

You are learning.

You are taller.

Going, Seeing, and Doing

1. Get a ⟨measuring tape⟩ .
   Go to a friend.
   Find out how tall your friend is.
   Find out how tall you are.
   Tell who is taller.
   Tell how much taller.

2. Watch some very young children.
   In what ways will they grow?

3. What do you want to learn to do?
   Find pictures of these things.
   Put the pictures together.
   Make a book.
   Give your book a name.

Helping Yourself Grow

You can help yourself grow.

Learn ways to stay well.

Eat food that is good for you.

Rest and sleep when you should.

Exercise every day.

Keep clean.

Work and play where it is safe.

Look at the pictures.

What are the people doing?

How are they helping themselves grow?

Can you help yourself grow?

Tell some things you can do.

Show some things you can do.

Others Help You Grow

Other people can help you grow.

Be a good listener.

Listen at school.

Teachers can help you learn.

Listen at home.

Your family can help you, too.

Be ready to learn.

Learning is a way of growing.

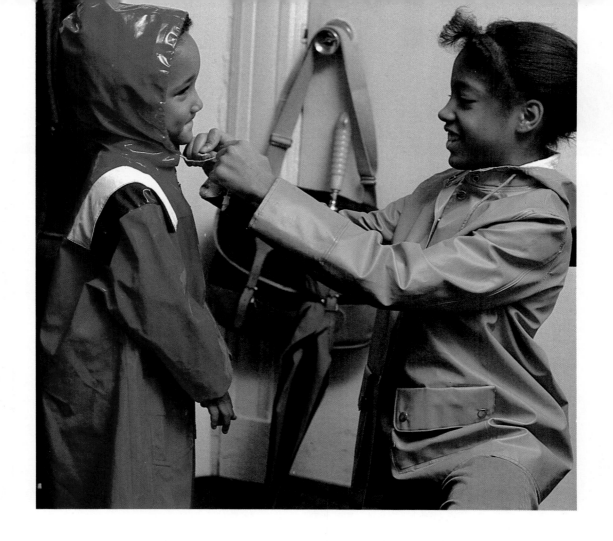

Look at the picture on page 30.
What are the children learning?
Who is helping them?

Look at the boy on this page.
He asked his sister for help.
How is she helping him?
Who can help you grow?

Your Turn

What Should Mike Do?

Kim and Tom are playing.

They have made animals.

Mike wants to make an animal, too.

He is trying very hard.

Things are not going very well.

What can Mike do to help himself?

Who else could help him?

What would you do?

Health in Action

1. Your teacher will point.
    Name the part of the body.
    Then, write the name.
    Use your own paper.

2. Plant a seed.
    Help it grow.
    Tell how you are helping.

3. Help yourself grow.
    Think of things you can do.
    Write them on paper.
    Do those things every day.

4. Copy the poem.
    Use your own paper.
    Then, finish the lines.

A baby is sm_____
But I am_____

Do You Remember?

Your Health Words

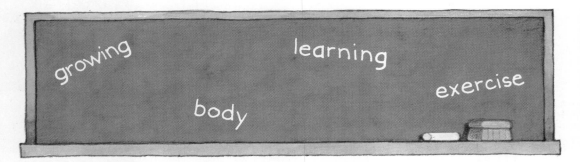

Answer the questions.
Use the Health Words.

1. What is your body doing?
2. What grows in many ways?
3. What helps you grow?

Your Health Ideas

1. Tell a way people grow bigger.
2. Tell a way people grow up.
3. List ways others help you grow.
4. Tell ways to help yourself grow.

Health Check-Up

Answer "Yes" or "No."

1. Are you growing smaller?
2. Is your whole body growing?
3. Does learning help you grow?
4. Can a baby do more than you?
5. Can you help yourself grow?
6. Is exercise bad for you?
7. Can you learn from teachers?
8. Can your family help you grow?

CHAPTER 3

Eating for Good Health

You need food every day.
You need the right kinds of food.
They help you stay well.
They help you grow.
They help you run and play.
Why do you need food?

Health Words

meals	lunch
breakfast	supper
energy	snacks

Foods for Growing

There are many kinds of food.

Some are milk and cheese.

Some are fruits and vegetables.

Others are meats and beans.

Still others are breads and cereals.

You need each kind of food every day.

Have them for meals.

They can help you stay healthy.

Look at all four pictures.
Name the foods.

Which foods have you tried?
Which would you like to try?
What is important about foods?
Which foods do you need every day?

Good Eating Habits

Eat foods that are good for you.

Enjoy your meals.

Take your time.

Sit down when you are eating.

Be sure your hands are clean.

Don't talk and eat at the same time.

Don't drink with food in your mouth.

Good eating habits are important.

They can help you stay healthy.

Look at all four pictures.
Name the good eating habits.
Tell why they are important.

Name other good eating habits.
Tell why they are important.

Health Highlight

Finding Good Eating Habits

Find the paths for good health.
Look for good eating habits.

Going, Seeing, and Doing

1. Find pictures of food.
   Bring them to school.
   Show your pictures.
   Name the foods you know.
   Ask about the others.

2. Act out a good eating habit.
   Don't tell what it is.
   Let others guess.

3. Make something good to eat.
   Read the recipe.
   Do what it says.
   Ask for help.
   Then, taste.

   Get these.

   SUNFLOWER SEEDS

   SHELLED NUTS

   Granola NO SUGAR NO SALT

   Do this. →

Eating Breakfast

Start your day off right.

Eat a good breakfast.

A good breakfast gives you energy.

You need energy to run and play.

You need energy to think.

A good breakfast helps you grow.

It helps you stay well.

Breakfast is an important meal.

Eat a good one every day.

Look at the breakfasts.

Name the foods.

Name other good breakfast foods.

Look at the children.

It is morning.

They had a good breakfast.

How can you tell?

Tell why breakfast is important.

Eating Lunch and Supper

You need energy all day long.

A good lunch can give you energy.

A good supper can, too.

Eat a good lunch and supper.

Eat different foods.

Eat foods that can help you stay well.

Eat foods that can help you grow.

Good food is part of good health.

Look at all three pictures.

What are the people eating?

Are these good meals?

How do you know?

What is a good meal?

Why are good meals important?

Eating Healthful Snacks

There are many snack foods.

You hear about them.

You see them in stores.

Some snack foods are good for you.

Fruit makes a good snack.

So do vegetables.

Candy is not good for you.

Think before you ask for a snack.

Be sure your snacks are good for you.

Look at the pictures on page 48.

Who is telling about a good snack?

How do you know?

Look at the pictures on this page.

What snack is the boy having?

What are the girls having?

Name some other good snack foods.

Your Turn

Carol's Snack

Carol just came home from school.
She wants to have a snack.
She does not know what to eat.

Help Carol pick a snack.
Name a good snack.
Tell why it is a good snack.

Health in Action

1. Think of a good meal.
    Find pictures of the foods.
    Paste the pictures on paper.
    Tell about your meal.

2. Taste some different foods.
    List the ones you like.
    List the ones you don't like.

3. Think of a good snack.
    Draw a picture of it.
    Tell why it is a good snack.

4. Write about breakfast.
    Tell about a good breakfast.
    Tell why breakfast is important.

Do You Remember?

Your Health Words

Finish the sentences.
Use the Health Words.

1. Start the day off right with ___.
2. Eating right gives me ___.
3. ___ are foods I eat between meals.

Your Health Ideas

1. Tell some good eating habits.
2. Name some different kinds of food.
3. Tell why people need good meals.
4. Tell what makes a good snack.

Health Check-Up

Answer "Yes" or "No."

1. Are all foods vegetables?
2. Do you need different foods?
3. Is it healthy to walk as you eat?
4. Is it healthy to eat slowly?
5. Is a good breakfast important?
6. Does breakfast give you energy?
7. Is lunch an important meal?
8. Are all snacks good for you?

CHAPTER 4

Caring About Your Teeth

You need your teeth.

They help you eat.

They help you have a nice smile.

They help you in other ways.

Take care of your teeth.

Help keep them healthy.

How can you care for your teeth?

Health Words

front teeth

back teeth

baby teeth

permanent teeth

brush

floss

dentists

55

Using Your Teeth

All your teeth are not the same.
Your front teeth are sharp.
They help you bite into food.
Your back teeth are wide.
They help you chew.
You need these different teeth.
Help them stay healthy.

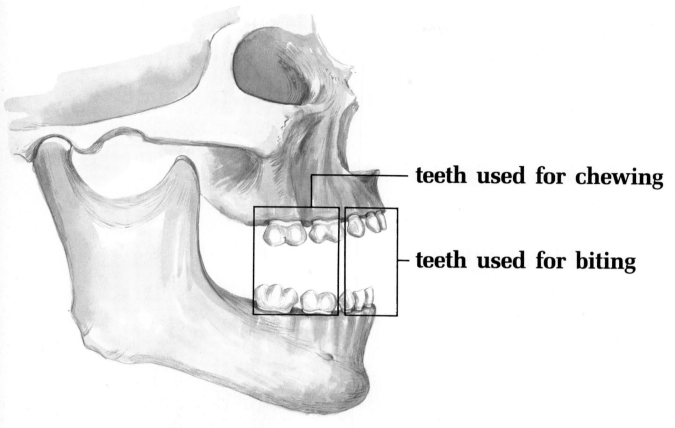

teeth used for chewing

teeth used for biting

Look at the boy.

Which teeth is he using?

How do you know?

Look at the teeth on this page.

Point to the front teeth.

Point to the back teeth.

How do teeth help you?

Your Two Sets of Teeth

Your first teeth are baby teeth.
They grew in when you were small.
Soon, you may begin to lose them.
You may have lost some already.
Other teeth will grow in.
These are your permanent teeth.
Take care of all your teeth.

Look at both pictures.

Point to the baby teeth.

Who is getting permanent teeth?

Tell why.

Health Highlight

Facts About Teeth

Finish each sentence.
Pick the best word.
Write the word.
Use your own paper.

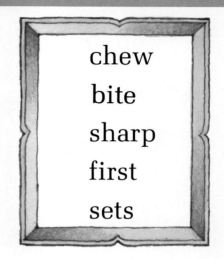

chew

bite

sharp

first

sets

1. My _ _ _ _ _ teeth are baby teeth.
2. I use my back teeth to _ _ _ _.
3. I have two _ _ _ _ of teeth.
4. My front teeth _ _ _ _ into food.
5. My front teeth are _ _ _ _ _.

Now, look at the letters of each word.
Find each letter that goes in a ◯.
What word do the letters make?

Going, Seeing, and Doing

1. Go to a  .
   Look at your teeth.
   Which are baby teeth?
   Which are permanent teeth?

2. Eat an apple.
   Look at yourself.
   Which teeth do you use?
   How do you use them?

3. Use clay.
   Make some teeth.
   Make front teeth.
   Make back teeth.

Helping Your Teeth Every Day

Take care of your teeth.

Don't eat sweets between meals.

Brush after eating.

Brush before bedtime.

Learn how to floss your teeth.

Floss every day.

Your teeth are important.

Help keep them healthy.

 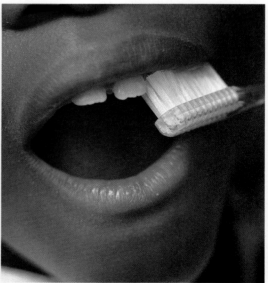

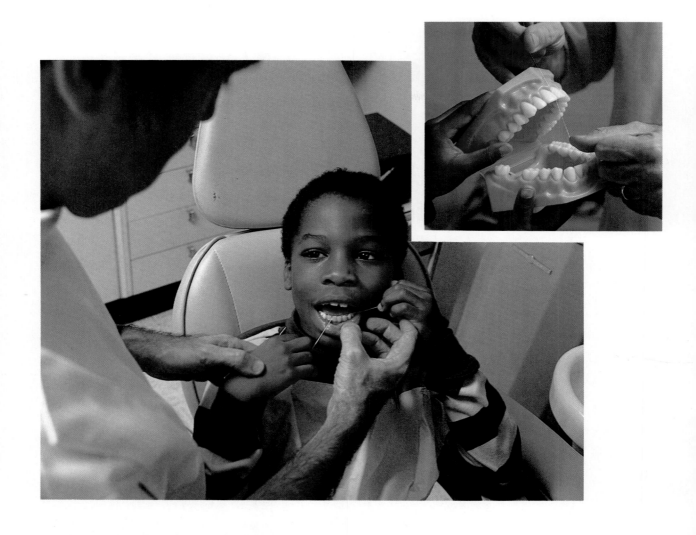

Look at the teeth.
How should you brush them?
When should you brush them?

Look at the boy.
What is he learning to do?
Why are clean teeth important?

Other Help for Your Teeth

Dentists can help your teeth.
They check for many things.
Are your teeth healthy?
Do they fit together?
Are they clean?
Dentists can find the answers.
Listen to what they say.
Do what they tell you to do.

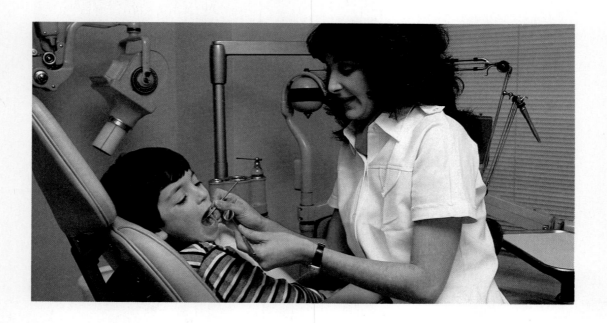

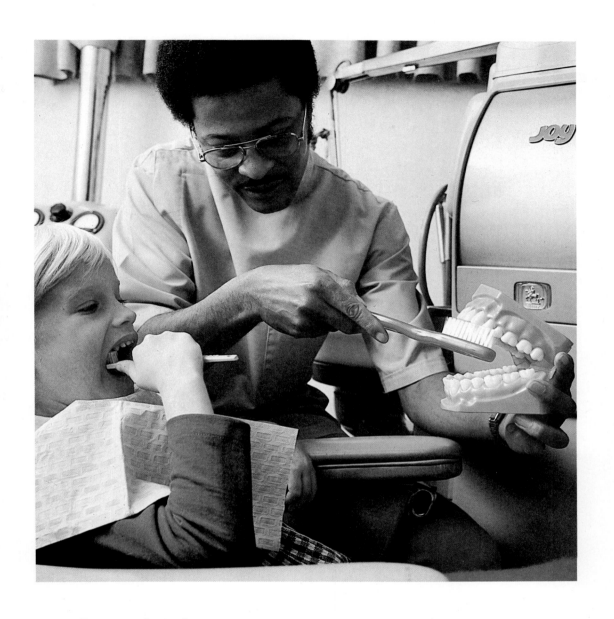

Look at both pictures.

How are the dentists helping?

Tell other ways dentists can help.

Tell how you can help.

Your Turn

After Lunch

Luis just ate lunch.
Now he is washing up.
He has washed his hands.
He has washed his face.

What else should Luis do?
Tell how your ideas would help.

Health in Action

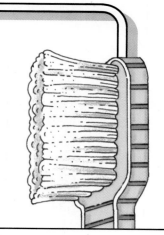

1. Make believe you have a ———.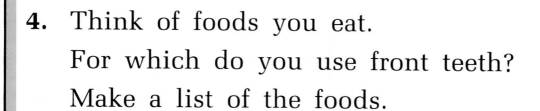
   Show how to brush your teeth.
   Show the right way.

2. Learn how to floss.
   Ask for help.

| After Breakfast |
| After Lunch |
| After Supper |
| After Snacks |
| Before Bed |

3. Copy the chart.
   Brush your teeth.
   Give yourself a ★.
   Put it on the chart.
   Brush often.
   Give yourself a ★ each time.

4. Think of foods you eat.
   For which do you use front teeth?
   Make a list of the foods.

Do You Remember?

Your Health Words

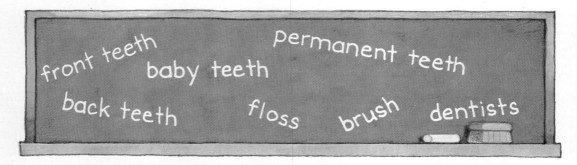

front teeth   baby teeth   permanent teeth

back teeth   floss   brush   dentists

Answer the questions.
Use the Health Words.

1. Which teeth are used for chewing?
2. Which are your second set of teeth?
3. What should you do after eating?
4. Who should check your teeth?

Your Health Ideas

1. Tell how teeth help you eat.
2. Show ways you can help your teeth.
3. Tell how dentists help your teeth.

Health Check-Up

Answer "Yes" or "No."

1. Do you use your teeth to eat?
2. Are front teeth used for chewing?
3. Do you have four sets of teeth?
4. Do you lose your baby teeth?
5. Do permanent teeth come in first?
6. Are your back teeth wide?
7. Should you brush after you eat?
8. Can dentists help your teeth?

CHAPTER 5

Staying Healthy

Staying well is many things.
It is taking care of yourself.
It is learning about your health.
It is getting the help you need.
You can help yourself every day.
What can you do to stay well?

Health Words

healthy	doctors
germs	nurses
cough	health helpers
sneeze	hospital

heart

Helping Yourself Stay Well

You can help yourself stay well.

Keep warm.

Dress for the day.

Wear rain clothes on wet days.

Wear warm clothes on cold days.

Stay healthy every day.

Look at the children.

What are they doing?

Are they dressed for the day?

How can you tell?

Helping Others Stay Well

Germs live all over.

Some even live inside people.

Some germs can make people ill.

Cover your mouth when you cough.

Do the same for sneezes.

Use a tissue.

Then, throw it away.

Help others stay well.

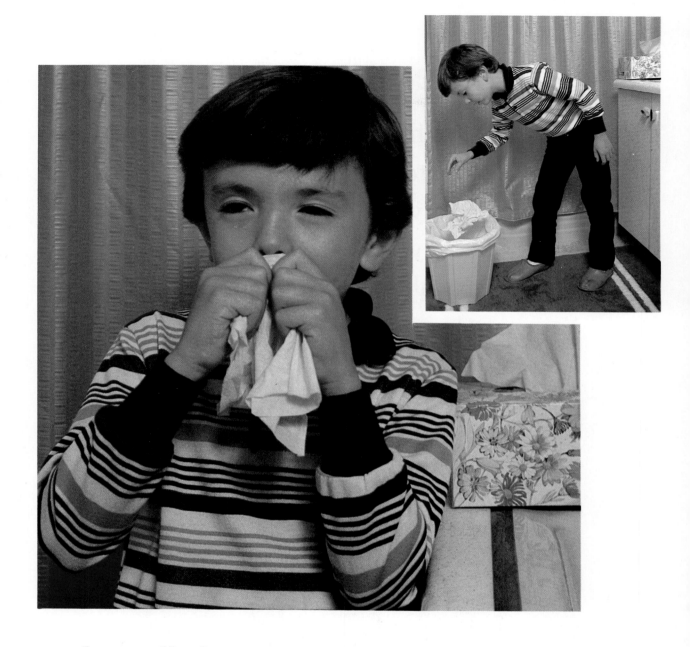

Look at all three pictures.
What are the children doing?
How are they helping others?
Tell other ways to help.

Your Health Helpers

Doctors are health helpers.

Nurses are, too.

They check your eyes.

They check your ears.

They learn about your health.

You can learn, too.

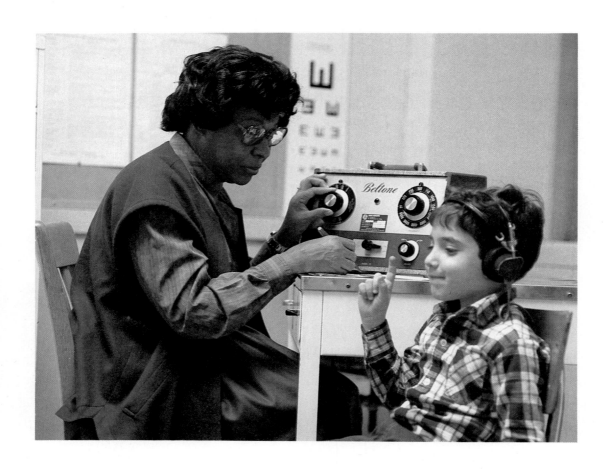

Look at the girl.
Is the nurse helping?
How?

Look at the boy.
How is the nurse helping?
Who else can help?
How can they help?

Following Directions

Doctors can help you in many ways.

Nurses can, too.

You can also help.

Ask them about your health.

Listen.

Do what they say.

Help your health helpers.

Help yourself.

Look at the boy and the doctor.
What is the boy learning?
How is the doctor helping?

Look at the boy on this page.
Did he follow the doctor's directions?
How can you tell?

Health Highlight

Staying Well and Helping Others

Look at the pictures.
Which ones go together?

1.

2.

3.

A.

B.

C.

Going, Seeing, and Doing

1. Go to the window.
   What is it like outside?
   Tell what you should wear.

2. Look at the picture.
   What is the doctor checking?
   Who else can check?
   What else can they do?

3. Help others stay well.
   Show some things you can do.

Hospitals Help, Too

The hospital is a special place.

Doctors work there.

Nurses work there.

They can give special help.

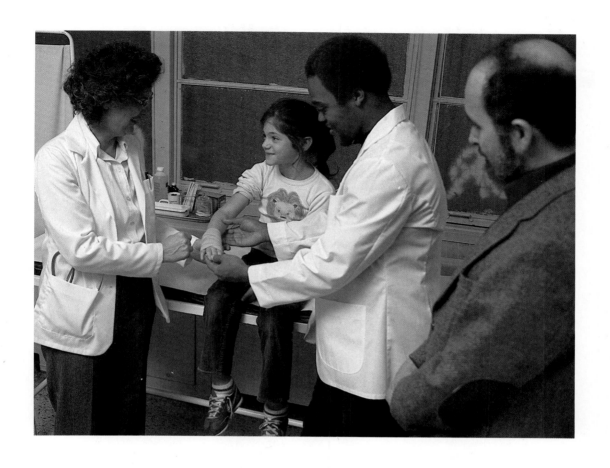

Look at the picture on page 82.
The girl is with her father.
Where is the girl going?

Look at the picture on this page.
Does the girl feel better?
How can you tell?
Tell how hospitals can help.

Your Turn

Can Ellen Come Out to Play?

Ellen has a cold.
Her two friends have come by.
They want to play.

Tell what Ellen should do.

Health in Action

1. Look at the germs.
   Where might you find them?
   What can some germs do?

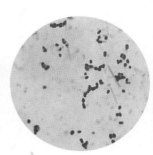

2. Tell who your health helpers are.
   In what ways can they help you?
   How can you help yourself?

3. Look at the clothes.
   Which are for rainy days?
   Which are for cold days?

4. Make a list.
   Tell how doctors can help you.
   Tell how hospitals can help.

Do You Remember?

Your Health Words

nurses   health helpers   cough

doctors   sneeze

healthy   hospital   germs

Finish the sentences.
Use the Health Words.

1. _____ can help you stay well.
2. _____ can give you a cold.
3. Cover your mouth when you _____.

Your Health Ideas

1. Tell ways to help yourself stay well.
2. Show how to help others stay well.
3. Tell how doctors can help.
4. Tell what can make people ill.

Health Check-Up

Answer "Yes" or "No."

1. Should you dress for the weather?
2. Can you help yourself stay well?
3. Is a doctor a health helper?
4. Can a nurse check your eyes?
5. Should you always wear warm clothes?
6. Should you listen to your doctor?
7. Should you save a used tissue?
8. Can hospitals give special help?

CHAPTER 6

Medicines and Your Health

Sometimes you may not feel well.

You may need help.

There are many kinds of help.

Find out what they are.

Learn about them.

Who can help you learn?

Health Words

medicines

pills

check-up

Help from Medicines

There are many medicines.

Some can help keep you well.

You may get these at a check-up.

Some can help you get well.

They can help fight germs.

They can help you feel better.

Medicine can help some of the time.

It does not help all of the time.

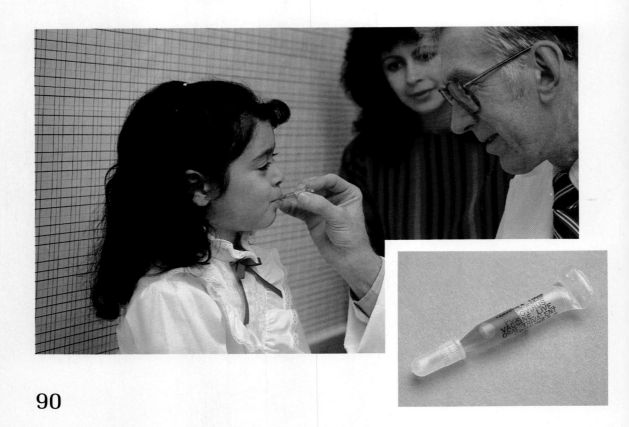

Look at the pictures.

Who is giving medicine?

How can the medicine help?

Tell other ways medicine can help.

Different Kinds of Medicine

Some medicines are pills.

Some are sprays.

Some are creams.

There are other kinds, too.

Learn about medicines.

Learn how they can help.

Learn when they can help.

Learn when they do not help.

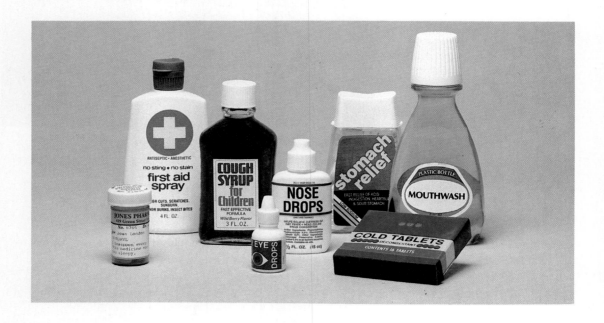

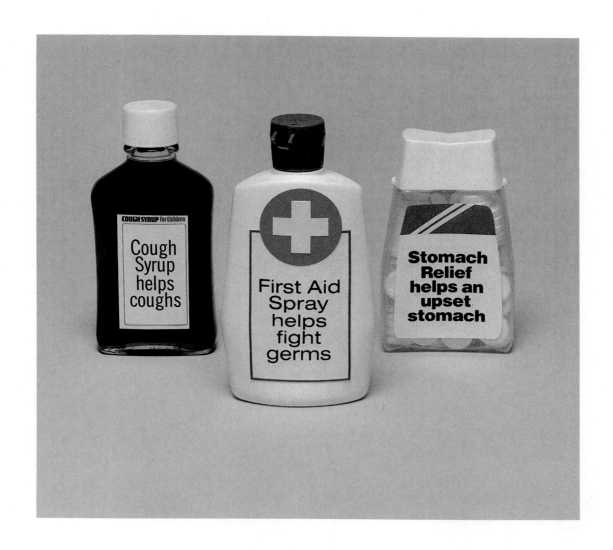

Cough Syrup helps coughs

First Aid Spray helps fight germs

Stomach Relief helps an upset stomach

Look at the medicines.
Which kinds do you see?

Look at the medicines above.
Try to read the words.
Tell how the medicine can help.

Getting Help with Medicine

Never take medicine on your own.

Never use it on your own.

Ask for help.

Ask your mother or father.

Ask other grown-ups in your family.

They can help you with medicine.

They may know if you need it.

They can give it to you if you do.

Look at both children.

Who is giving them medicine?

Who can help you use medicine?

Health Highlight

Who Can Help with Medicine?

Copy the letters in each row.
Read the words.
Use them to answer the question.
Who should give you medicine?

```
1 2 n u 7 9 r 6 s e
f 7 4 r i e 8 n 5 d
5 g r 3 a n d 2 m a
2 d 1 o c 3 t o r 7
9 6 8 m o t 5 h e r
g 3 r a 7 n d p a 2
f a 2 t h 6 3 e 8 r
0 b 2 a 8 3 5 b 7 y
6 w 9 2 a 4 i t e r
```

Going, Seeing, and Doing

1. Look around your home.
   Go with a grown-up.
   Find medicines.
   Put them in a safe place.

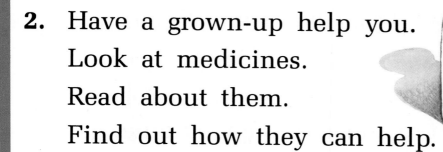

2. Have a grown-up help you.
   Look at medicines.
   Read about them.
   Find out how they can help.

3. Who can help you with medicine?
   Draw a picture.
   Show someone who can help.
   Then, tell who it is.

Medicine May Not Be Needed

Medicine does not always help.

You may not always need it.

Sometimes just resting helps.

Food that is good for you can help.

Exercise can help, too.

These are good habits.

Make them your habits.

Good habits can be good medicine.

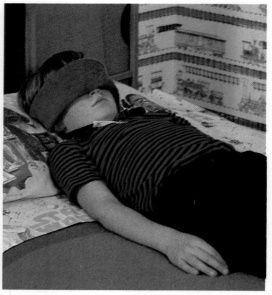

Look at the pictures on the left.
Did the boy take medicine?
What did he do?

Look at the other picture.
Does the boy feel better?
What could have helped him?
Tell other things that can help.

Your Turn

Ways to Rest

Tony does not feel well.
He needs to rest.
He is not sleepy, though.

Help Tony.
Tell some things he can do.
Name some quiet games.
Tell how they could help.

Health in Action

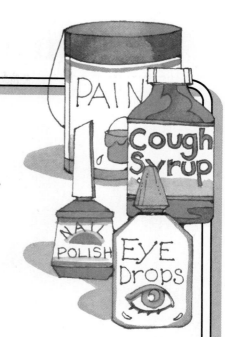

1. Look at the pictures.
   Tell which are medicines.

2. Tell about medicines.
   What kinds are there?
   What can they do?

3. Whom should you ask about medicine?
   Make a list.
   Then, write some questions to ask.

4. Answer the questions in the box.
   Write the answers on paper.

   How can medicines help you?
   What can help besides medicine?

Do You Remember?

Your Health Words

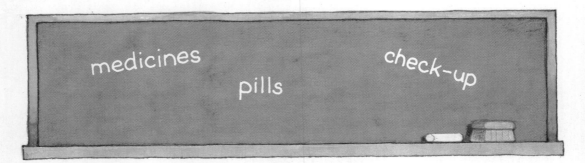

Finish the sentences.
Use the Health Words.

1. Some _____ can fight germs.
2. Don't take _____ by yourself.
3. You may get medicine at a _____.

Your Health Ideas

1. Tell what medicines can do.
2. Name some kinds of medicine.
3. Tell who knows about medicine.
4. Tell what can help besides medicine.

Health Check-Up

Answer "Yes" or "No."

1. Can medicines always help?
2. Can a nurse give you medicine?
3. Can you get medicine at check-ups?
4. Are all medicines pills?
5. Are all medicines the same?
6. Should friends give you medicine?
7. Can some medicine fight germs?
8. Might resting help you feel better?

CHAPTER 7

Actions for Safety

You can do things safely.
Walk and ride safely.
Play and work safely.
Be careful around strangers.
Do things safely all the time.
It can help you stay healthy.
Why should you do things safely?

Health Words

corners   seatbelt
crosswalks   poisons
traffic   strangers
safety

BICYCLE INSPECTIONS

105

Crossing a Street Safely

You can cross a street safely.

Cross at corners.

Cross where you see crosswalks.

Look both ways before you cross.

Watch for traffic.

Watch the traffic light.

Cross only when it is green.

Cross only when cars have stopped.

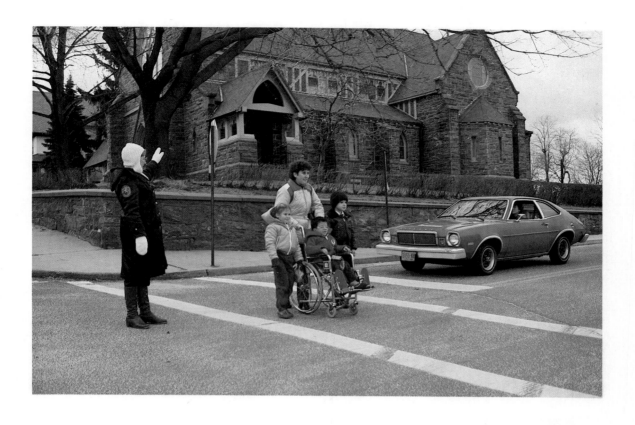

Look at the traffic lights.
Name the colors.
What does each tell you to do?

Look at the children.
Are they crossing safely?
How can you tell?
Who is helping them cross safely?
How can you cross safely?

Riding a Bicycle Safely

You can ride a bicycle safely.

Ride a safe bicycle.

Watch out for cars and people.

Watch out for holes in the road.

Ride behind or in front of others.

Don't ride next to them.

Learn other bicycle safety rules.

Follow the rules every time you ride.

Look at the girls.

Are they riding safely?

How can you tell?

Look at the bicycle.

Is it a safe bicycle?

What makes it safe?

Tell some ways to ride safely.

Riding in Cars Safely

You can ride in cars safely.

Use a seatbelt.

Use it every time you ride.

Help the driver drive safely.

Talk quietly.

Play quiet games.

Help yourself stay safe.

Help others stay safe, too.

Look at the pictures on the left.

What is the boy doing?

When should you use seatbelts?

Look at the picture above.

Are the children riding safely?

Tell how you know.

Health Highlight

What Is Missing?

Look at each picture.
Tell what is missing.
Tell how it could help with safety.

Going, Seeing, and Doing

1. Go across a street.
Go with a grown-up.
Cross the street safely.

2. Watch people riding bicycles.
Are they riding bicycles safely?
How do you know?
Tell ways to ride safely.

3. Make believe you are in a car.
Tell how to ride safely.
Name a safe game for a car trip.

Playing Inside Safely

Think about safety as you play.

Play safely inside.

Play quiet games.

Play in safe places.

The floor can be a safe place.

Steps are not safe.

Clean up after you play.

Help keep yourself and others safe.

Look at the boy playing alone.
Is he playing safely?
Tell how you know.

Look at the other children.
Are they thinking about safety?
How can you tell?
Name a safe game to play inside.
How can you play safely inside?

Playing Outside Safely

You can play safely in many places.

Parks can be safe places to play.

Playgrounds can be, too.

Some places are not safe to play.

Streets are not.

Empty buildings are not.

Play only where you can play safely.

Always think about your safety.

Look at both pictures.

Where are the children playing?

Are these safe places to play?

How do you know?

Name other safe places to play.

Carrying Things Safely

Keep yourself from getting hurt.

Carry  with the cutting parts down.

Be careful carrying big things.

Be sure you can see around them.

If you can't, ask for help.

Don't carry many things at once.

Put some things down.

Make two trips.

Look at all the children.

Are they carrying things safely?

How can you tell?

Show how to carry  safely.

Show how to carry other things safely.

Being Careful Around Strangers

Strangers are people you don't know.

Sometimes they may talk to you.

They may want to give you things.

They may ask you to go with them.

Be careful.

Do not go with strangers.

Do not take things from them.

Help keep yourself safe.

Look at the children.

Are they acting safely?

How do you know?

How should you act with strangers?

Knowing What Can Be Harmful

Some things are safe.

Some things are not safe.

Poisons are not safe.

They can make you very ill.

Learn which things are poisons.

Learn which things are safe.

Learn to use things safely.

Ask a grown-up for help.

Look at all ten pictures.

Which things are safe to eat?

Which things are safe to drink?

Which are poisons?

Tell what poisons can do.

Tell how to keep yourself safe.

Your Turn

The Stranger

Tina is playing.

A stranger comes by in a car.

He tells Tina that he is lost.

He asks Tina to show him the way.

He tells Tina to get into the car.

Help Tina.

Tell what she should do.

Tell why.

Health in Action

1. Look at the pictures.
   How would you carry each thing?
   Show what you would do.

2. Cut out pieces of green paper.
   Then go around your home.
   Go with a grown-up.
   Find poisons.
   Glue green paper on each one.

3. Draw a traffic light.
   Color it in.
   Tell what the colors mean.

4. Where can you play safely?
   Make a list of some places.

Do You Remember?

Your Health Words

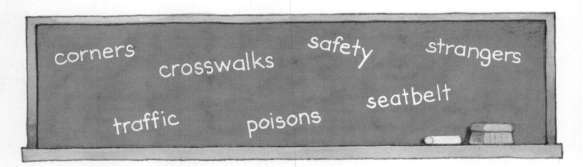

corners
crosswalks
safety
strangers
seatbelt
traffic
poisons

Finish the sentences.
Use the Health Words.

1. ____ are people you do not know.
2. ____ are safe places to cross a street.
3. Use a ____ when you ride in a car.

Your Health Ideas

1. Tell ways to walk and ride safely.
2. Tell where you can play safely.
3. Tell what to do around strangers.
4. Show how to carry things safely.

Health Check-Up

Answer "Yes" or "No."

1. Does a red light mean go?
2. Does a safe bicycle have a bell?
3. Should you use a seatbelt?
4. Is it safe to play on steps?
5. Is the street a safe place to play?
6. Should you run as you carry  ?
7. Should you go with strangers?
8. Are poisons good for you?

CHAPTER 8

Caring About Your World

We all live in the same world.
We can all help take care of it.
We can help keep it clean.
We can help keep it healthful.
Everyone can work together.
We can each do our part.
What can you do to help?

Health Words

environment

water

litter

trash

Being a Leader

Your environment is all around you.

You work in it.

You play in it.

You share it with others.

Help your environment.

Help take care of it.

What you do is important.

You can make a difference.

Look at the people.

Are they helping their environment?

How do you know?

Tell about your environment.

How can you help take care of it?

Why should you help?

Saving Water

Our water comes from rain and snow.

Sometimes it rains and snows a lot.

Sometimes it does not.

We always need water, though.

We need it every day.

We need water to live.

We need it to stay healthy.

Help save water.

Use only what you need.

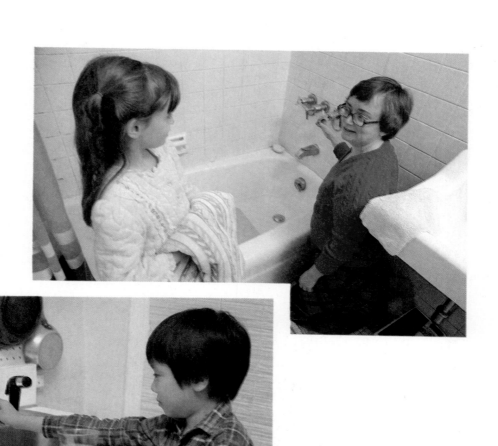

Look at all three pictures.

Which shows where water is stored?

Which show ways to help save water?

How else can you save water?

Why should you help save water?

Cleaning Up Outside

Trash is what you throw away.
Litter is a kind of trash.
It is trash left on the ground.
It is not safe to play in litter.
It is not healthful to be around it.
Put your trash in a trash can.
Clean up after you play.
Help keep yourself safe.
Help keep yourself healthy.

Point to the litter.
How does it make things look?

Look at the children.
What are they doing?
How are they helping the outdoors?
What can you do to help?
Why should you help?

Health Highlight

You Can Make a Difference

Look at the picture.

Make believe you are on the path.

Walk along it.

Tell what you see.

Tell what needs to be done.

Going, Seeing, and Doing

1. Go into your home.
    Go with a grown-up.
    Walk from room to room.
    Find out ways to save water.
    Tell about the ways.

2. Watch on your way home.
    Do you see trash cans?
    Why should you use them?

3. How can you help outdoors?
    Think of something you can do.
    Draw a picture to show it.

Cleaning Up Inside

You can help take care of things.

Clean up after you eat.

Clean up after you play.

Put trash in a wastebasket.

Help keep things looking nice.

A clean environment is important.

It helps you feel good.

It helps you stay healthy.

Look at the children.
Are they helping?
How?
How else can they help?

Is a clean environment important?
Why?

Your Turn

After the Party

Pete's party is over.
Food and dishes are on the table.
Toys are on the floor.
Pete wants to play.
Should Pete play?

What should he do?

Health in Action

1. Make a small trash can.
    Paint it a color you like.
    Paint the word "trash" on it.
    Take it home and use it.

2. How can you help outdoors?
    Make a list of some ways.

3. How can you help indoors?
    Show a way.
    Don't say what it is.
    Let others guess.

4. Write a story.
    Begin it this way:
    "I know how to save water."

Do You Remember?

Your Health Words

Finish the sentences.
Use the Health Words.

1. You need _____ to stay healthy.
2. Help take care of your _____.
3. It is not safe to play with _____.

Your Health Ideas

1. Tell why you should save water.
2. Tell how to care for the indoors.
3. Tell how to care for the outdoors.

Health Check-Up

Answer "Yes" or "No."

1. Do you share your environment?
2. Is litter pretty?
3. Do people need water every day?
4. Is it silly to save water?
5. Should you clean up after eating?
6. Should you put trash on the floor?
7. Should you help clean up inside?
8. Can you help keep parks clean?

Exercise Handbook

Exercise is good for you.

It can help you stay well.

It can help you look and feel good.

Ask your doctor about exercises.

Find out which ones are best for you.

Do them every day.

Stretching Out

Do stretching exercises first.

Stretch your arms and legs.

Stretch all your muscles.

Get them warmed up.

Get them ready for other exercises.

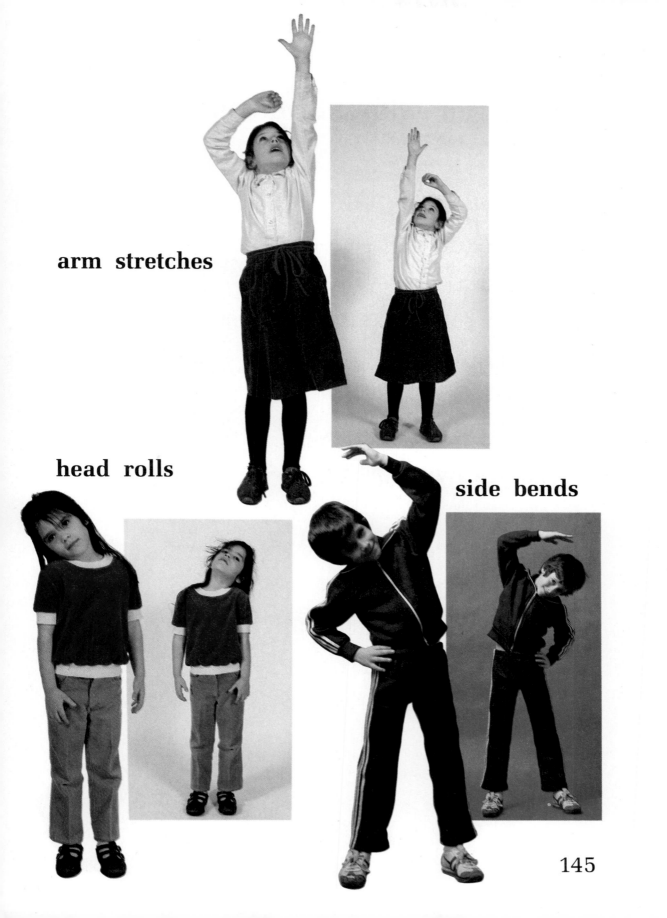

arm stretches

head rolls

side bends

145

Having Fun with Movement

You can exercise alone.

You can exercise with others.

Getting exercise can be fun.

Always start by stretching.

Then, do other exercises.

Move about.

Jump or skip.

Play a running game.

Play a throwing game.

Swim.

Dance.

Ride a bicycle.

Exercise helps your heart.

It helps keep your heart healthy.

It helps keep you healthy.

Cooling Down

Don't stop moving all at once.
First, slow down.
Do some stretching exercises.
Walk around.
Shake your arms and hands.
Breathe deeply.
Do other easy exercises.
Do them slowly.
Then, stop and rest.

knee lifts

arm circles

deep breathing

Reviewing the HEALTH WORDS

The health words in the list are from the first page of each chapter.
After each word is its meaning. Then, the word is used in a sentence.
The number in dark print tells where to find the word in the book.

B

baby teeth, the first set of teeth that grows in. Beth lost her first two baby teeth when she was seven. **58**

back teeth, the teeth used for chewing food. Sara uses her back teeth to chew. **56**

body, all of the parts that make up a person. Adam's whole body is growing. **22**

breakfast, the first meal of the day. Julio had breakfast every day. **44**

brush, to clean teeth with a toothbrush. Pat tries to brush her teeth after eating. **62**

C

check-up, when a doctor or dentist looks at your body or teeth. The dentist cleaned Jason's teeth during the check-up. **90**

corner, the place where streets meet. Ling crossed a street only at the corner. **106**

crosswalk, the part of a street that is marked off for people to use when crossing. Hana crossed the street between the two lines of the crosswalk. **106**

cough, something often done when someone has a cold. Jonathan covered his mouth when he started to cough. **74**

D

dentist, a person who is trained to help take care of the teeth. The dentist told Grace that her teeth were healthy. **64**

doctor, a person who is trained to give health care. The doctor took care of the cut on David's foot. **76**

E

energy, the power to do things. Karen always has energy to play. **44**

environment, everything that is around you. Many people share the same environment. **130**

exercise, a way of moving the body to help keep it healthy. Roger's favorite kind of exercise is swimming. **28**

F

family, the people who live together in a home. Fran and her family moved to a new home. **14**

feelings, happy, sad, and afraid are kinds of feelings. Rob named some feelings he likes to have. **6**

floss, to use a special kind of string to clean between the teeth. The school nurse showed Elizabeth how to floss her teeth. **62**

friends, people who like one another. Anna and her friends have fun. **12**

front teeth, the teeth used to bite into food. Alex bit into the apple with his front teeth. **56**

G

germs, tiny, living things. Some germs can make people ill. **74**

growing, getting bigger. Dave is growing taller. **22**

H

habit, something that is done without thinking about it. Ben has a habit of exercising everyday. **8**

health helpers, people who are trained in health care. Doctors, dentists, and nurses are health helpers. **76**

healthy, not ill. Jack felt good because he was healthy. **72**

hospital, a place where people can go for health care. Jody went to the hospital after she fell. **82**

L

learning, finding out about something. Kevin was learning how to swim. **30**

litter, trash that is left lying on the ground. Barbara put some litter in a trash can. **134**

lunch, a meal often eaten in the middle of the day. Greg had a chicken sandwich, grapes, and milk for lunch. **46**

M

meals, food that is eaten at certain times during the day. Breakfast, lunch, and supper are three meals. **47**

medicine, something that can help fight illness. Gloria's mother gave her some cough medicine. **90**

N

nurse, a person trained to give some kinds of health care. The nurse took Bill's temperature. **76**

P

permanent teeth, the second set of teeth that grows in. Nancy has three permanent teeth. **58**

pill, a form in which medicine comes. Ricky swallowed a pill his mom gave him. **92**

poison, something that can be very harmful if swallowed. Mr. Romero put the poison on a high shelf. **122**

S

safety, not being in danger. Theresa thought about her safety when she crossed the street. **108**

seatbelt, the strap in a car that holds a person in the seat. Linda buckled her seatbelt as soon as she got in the car. **110**

snack, a food that is eaten between meals. Bob's favorite snack was grapes. **48**

sneeze, something often done when someone has a cold. Lila used a tissue when she began to sneeze. **74**

special, something or someone important. Everyone is special. **4**

strangers, people you do not know. Hal doesn't speak to strangers. **120**

supper, a meal often eaten in the evening. The Tagawa family has supper together every night. **46**

T

traffic, the cars, trucks, and buses that move along a street. Judy watches for traffic when she rides her bicycle. **106**

trash, things that are thrown away. Larry put his trash in a basket. **138**

W

water, something that everyone needs to live. Jeanette's favorite drink is cold water. **132**

Index

154

E
F
G
H
I
J